THE BUSINESS OF LIFE AND GOLF

PATRICK M GASKILL

CONTENTS

THE BUSINESS OF LIFE AND GOLF

"A master in the art of living draws no sharp distinction between their work and their play; their labor and their leisure; their mind and their body; their education and their recreation. They hardly know which is which. They simply pursue their vision of excellence through whatever they are doing, and leave others to determine whether they are working or playing. To themselves, they always appear to be doing both."

L.P. Jacks

INTRODUCTION

This book contains, in part, what I have learned and observed about Club Membership over the past 12 years. This is meant to be a guide for you if you are considering Club Membership or, if you are already a Member of a Club, you may think this book should have been issued to you as an orientation and a guide as to how best enjoy your time at your Club.

I wanted to express my gratitude for the experience we have had and provide a platform to spur discussion among Club Members about some topics that are sometimes tough to talk about. Joining a Club has been one of the most rewarding experiences of our lives and I wish many, many more people would enjoy the experience as we have. There are many misperceptions, some negative stereotypes and outdated views about Golf Club Membership and this book is going to address some of those head on.

We've all heard some version of "more business gets done on the golf course than anywhere else". This book started with the concept of digging into that and helping people consider Golf in their Business. However, the more I wrote, the less I wanted to write about the Business aspect and the more I wanted to write a guidebook of sorts to Club Membership itself.

In this book, we are going to finally address that line of thinking in the proper way. For the record, I've seen very little business get done "on the golf course". My bio would include being a Financial Advisor for over 20 years, a CFP since 2005 and a Coach for over 100 other Financial Advisors and their clients for over 15 years. We've been Members at Somersett Golf and Country Club since 2008. I have served on various Committees and a few years as President of the Board, so I got a good look at a lot of dynamics going on; membership growth challenges in particular. More on that challenge later.

My wife, Sheri, and I did not grow up in Clubs or around golf at all, but our kids did. More on having the kids get involved in the game later too. Sheri picked up the game as well and is getting pretty good at it. I started playing in my late 20's with some guys from work. Looking back, what a miserable experience playing golf with me must have been! I was horrible at it, as are most who first learn the game as adults. We got hooked on the game and eventually joined a Club thinking it would be good for family time and for business; as it turned out, it was good for both. Looking back, the decision of joining a golf club would have been well worth it without the business side at all, and I wish more people could experience what we have.

1

SO WHY JOIN A CLUB?

"...and if you play golf, you are my friend"
Harvey Penick

THE WELL-KNOWN HARVEY PENICK QUOTE MIGHT TRANSLATE TO THE fact that we have a common passion in life. That would be golf, and because of that and all that goes with it, we will likely get along. Of course, there are exceptions to that, but the concept remains for the most part that if you play golf, then you and I are "simpatico" even from the first time we meet until we find out otherwise. In other words, the default is that we're friends immediately, and don't underestimate that. That dynamic plays itself out at networking events, parties, corporate boardrooms and golf clubs all over the world and it's a BIG darn deal. It's the ultimate icebreaker and fast forward button for building relationships and making connections.

BEING a Club Member is a slightly different animal than just being a golfer. Yes, the amazing dynamic that exists among golfers is there, but on a magnified level. You see, I generally really like golfers, but I'd run through a brick wall for a fellow Club Member...and jump at the chance to do it. And many of them would do the same for you. I've seen it dozens and dozens of times at my Club. Tell me where you find THAT in your life. For most of us, we're very blessed if we have 1 or 2 good friends after high school and college in our lives and a handful or so of other friends that fill our lives with good times and great memories, as well as exciting things to look forward to together. If you have your health, some good friends and family, then you're a wealthy person. Golf Clubs are like planting yourself in a garden where relationships can grow, but it doesn't happen automatically for everyone as you would be wise to tend to that garden. You'll get out of it what you put into it. See Chapter 3 on How to be a Great Club Member.

HERE'S THE THING, I'm in the money business. Financial Advisor, CFP, Wealth Manager etc. But who is REALLY wealthy anyway and how do we measure that? Net Worth? That just means you have money. I must tell you that I don't think that's the best measurement of wealth. I've been working with Clients and Coaching Financial Advisors to work with their clients for over 20 years now. My thoughts on this have changed over the years and here's what I think in general terms. Once a person has enough dough to be comfortable plus a little more, then that side of the wealth meter gets a check mark in the box. You have money. Check the box. You don't necessarily get extra check marks for each million above that, or each extra home above the one you live in or what type of cars are in the garage and so forth. Don't get me wrong, those other things are enjoyable and nice if you have them but there are many studies that show there is not a big jump in happiness once you're beyond a certain point. But that's not what really moves the needle, in my opinion. Just check that box as having enough money, and a little more; enough to pay your Club dues, vacation with friends, visit family, and help out in your community. From there, true wealth might just be in the relationships you have and in the joy of helping other people. I look at some of the people in my Club and spontaneously think to myself "that's a really wealthy person". But when I find myself thinking that it's almost NEVER about the money, it's how rich they are in friendships and relationships and it's because they are just such great people. I may or may not know anything at all about their Net Worth, but I can tell they are wealthy, the way that I see wealth, by the way they interact with their friends. That's what Clubs can do; they can help grow wealth as measured in relationships. That kind of wealth, the kind you may really want.

As a person who has served on Club Boards in various positions, a persistent problem in attracting new members has been the mindset of the potential Member trying to make a decision is that this was mostly a Math decision. How many times a month will I play divided into the monthly dues amount? Does the unlimited access to golf, great facilities and high standards of course maintenance justify my cost? Of course, there is a financial decision to be made in regard to the expense, but my sense is that the cost per round is given more weight than it should. That is completely understandable because the other benefits are somewhat intangible.

So why join a Club?

Maybe it's because you show up with some money but have a chance to become wealthy in relationships, camaraderie and experiences.

That's why you join a Club.

2

WE'RE NOT COUNTRY CLUB PEOPLE

"From the outside looking in, you can't understand it. From the inside looking out, we can't explain it" *Texas A&M trying to explain the Tradition that exists at the University*

WELL, LET ME TAKE A SHOT AT EXPLAINING IT. FOR THOSE WHO HAVE never belonged to a golf club and are considering it, it's not unusual to be thinking something along the lines of "we're not Country Club people". I've heard it many times over the years. The impression from the outside of who the people are in many Clubs tends to be somewhat outdated, stereotyped and inaccurate. There exists what I like to call "head trash". I first heard the term head trash in a professional sense about how we allow our thoughts and limiting beliefs to stop ourselves from reaching our potential. Basically, we defeat ourselves mentally before even getting started. Well, head trash is an obstacle that plays itself out as people consider Club Membership also and it's a big issue. The old stereotypes are stubborn and tend to stick in societies' mind.

. . .

THERE ARE many types of Clubs, and they range in character and culture. I hope you find a good fit for you. The fee for entry can vary widely and that usually is the biggest differentiator. Some Clubs can be joined for little or no money down and others require 6 figures, still others are even more exclusive and are by invitation only. The type of Club our family has been around could be described as a Middle-Class Club. Even that term "Middle-Class" has a pretty wide set of boundaries when it comes to income and net worth.

SHERI and I did not grow up in a Club environment. We came from what most anyone would agree were relatively modest backgrounds. Sheri's Dad was a high school teacher and her Mom was a homemaker. My parents were divorced at a very early age, my Mom and I then lived with my grandparents until I was 7. She joined the Air Force, we moved out and she married again when I was 16 to an exceptionally good man who also was in the Air Force. Looking back, I guess you could say we didn't have much money, but I would describe my childhood as an excellent one and looking back can't say money was important or missing at all, from my perspective. Maybe that's why I still believe that the bigger part of true wealth comes from friends and family relationships.

Do we fit the stereotype for Country Club Members? We did not hit the lottery, work for the right company where stock options changed our financial lives, or had a sudden wealth event of any sort. But a good career path provided enough money and a little extra. As we started raising our family, golf started to look like a good activity for us all to do together and it might be good for business too, so we started really thinking about it. We even talked about it as a parenting strategy of sorts. When our two daughters were very young, we were already thinking about the legendary teenage years to come that we had heard so much about. We literally said it out loud, "you know, when the 'you-know-what' hits the fan when they are teenagers, getting 4 or 5 hours together out on a golf course might be just enough glue to help get us through those tough years. We might need that time." The kids were probably only 4 and 1 at the time, but I'm a Planner for a living.

WE WEREN'T REALLY THINKING MUCH at all about the lasting friendships that would form. Fast forward and the teenage years weren't so bad, the girls turned out to be pretty good golfers, continued to play for their college teams, and we have a life-long sport we can all play and enjoy together as a family. Let me say that one again, we have a lifelong sport we can play and enjoy together!

So, if Sheri and I don't fit the Country Club people stereotype, are we the outliers? Are we so different than the other people at the Club? We don't think so. Now, we don't know everyone's background as kids for the most part but if I were to paint the picture of the stereotypical Club Member at our place there would be a few categories and they would look something like this...

THEY ARE, or were, successful at their careers, so they make enough money and a little more. They are small business owners, many in the medical field. They are Dentists, Optometrists, Surgeons, and such.There are a few Attorneys. If they work for a larger company, usually they have a mid-level or higher Management role, department head, CFO or run the Sales side of the organization in some way. We have School Teachers and Administrators. There are self-employed entrepreneurs, Realtors, Insurance Agents, Mortgage people, Financial Advisors. Lots of retired people too who may have been in those careers during their working lives.

ALL the above seem to work really hard, they have taken on bigger responsibilities than most, they have or had work stress, they've taken some risks and have found some success somehow along the way.

I ALSO WANT to note that most everyone we know at our Club seem to be really, really family oriented. They want what everyone wants, to be good parents and to raise decent kids. And they work at it. It's clear that it's important to them. I love that. And for those who fit that retired category and their kids are grown, you can tell how much it means to them when they do see their kids and grandkids.

WHO WOULDN'T WANT to be around people like this? And who wouldn't want their kids growing up around people like this? Ok, admittedly and stereotypically, there are a few who may have gotten a pretty good head start on the money side of things by virtue of who their parents or grandparents were and perhaps an even smaller number of those lack a little humility about that fact. But that would be a real rarity. Total opposite of what the Country Club stereotype may seem. In fact, there are many here who were afforded a head start in the money race I suppose who are very grounded about it. Not a pretentious bone in their bodies. And for the record, those folks generally still work hard too now, are successful at their careers, face the same stress levels in their jobs and over raising kids as anyone else and are terrific people. At least at our Club it seems that way.

I SUPPOSE ALL the above will vary by the type of Club you look to join. Find one that fits you and give it a chance. Don't let a bunch of head trash about who the people might be stop you before you get started.

3

HOW TO BE A GREAT CLUB MEMBER
IN 10 EASY STEPS

"You don't want your name on a Champagne Bottle"

A BIT STRANGE TO START A CHAPTER THAT WILL EMPHASIZE POSITIVE vibes all the time with an urban golf legend about how Clubs handle troublemakers. It involves a bottle of cheap champagne and a great deal of patience. The Golf Club business is a service business and sometimes service businesses have to deal with difficult customers. Rumor has it that one way the golf staff may cope with these difficult people, who have finally broken that last straw, was by writing their name on a bottle of champagne. And then they wait until the Member eventually leaves to pop the cork and celebrate their departure. You don't want your name on a champagne bottle.

HERE ARE 10 rules to follow to get you started on a great Club experience:

1. You are there to have a good time
2. Treat the staff with appreciation and respect
3. Choose to be positive

4. Don't be cheap
5. Be aware of a few common pitfalls
6. About alcohol
7. Play the big events
8. Connect on social media
9. Find a few regular golf buddies
10. Do business with your fellow club members if appropriate

Rule Number 1 - You Are There to Have a Good Time!

A few months after joining our Club, we heard someone trying to describe all the fun going on around here. I've repeated it many times to others and it was "it's kinda like being in college again, only now everybody has some money". Let the good times roll! There's something special in life about being around a bunch of people just having a good time. Don't over-think it, just go with it and you'll be glad you did. Say yes to lots of stuff. Say yes to the Social Events at your Club, say yes when someone invites you play golf, say yes to invites to fellow members parties that they may be hosting.

The Club can be your safe zone of sorts. You may have a ton of responsibilities at your job and you may have a certain persona that you have to maintain there. But that's the work you. The non-work you needs a place to call home too and that can be your golf club. Every time your tires hit that parking lot, I hope there's a little extra bounce in your step because you are entering the fun zone in your life. It's time to laugh, enjoy some cama-raderie and enjoy the characters all around you.

. . .

IF YOU FOLLOW Rule Number 1, then the rest of the rules tend to take care of themselves. But human nature being what it is with our ability to make uncomplicated things complicated, the other 9 rules are worth mentioning and then there is a special chapter later that is reserved for what happens on the golf course itself. 10 rules plus a bonus section, if you will.

RULE NUMBER 2 - Treat the Staff with Appreciation and Respect
The people working at these Clubs for the most part are really special people and it's best to know that right from the beginning. We did not know that when we joined but over the years have we learned to thoroughly enjoy their friendship and how much they mean to us in terms of how we view our Membership.

GET to know the staff people at your club for who they are, and you'll be glad you did. I can't speak for everyone, but for Sheri and I and our family, they are a critical part of our overall Club experience and enjoyment.

WHEN WE FIRST JOINED THE Club, we didn't know anyone. The Staff became our first friends and frankly a security blanket of sorts to make us feel just a little comfortable at least when we would come to the Club early on. There's an awkward period right after joining your new club. At least there was for us. You show up for the first time for a drink around happy hour and everyone seems to know each other, or at least they know someone and have someone to talk to. Except you. So, you do what comes natural when uncomfortable at a party and head straight for the bar and the bartender. Your first new friend! And the next time you come in, you have 1 friend in the room and it's that bartender and you feel great when she remembers your name and maybe even what you like to drink already. And so, it begins! It's like you and your Club have survived a first date.

DURING YOUR VISITS to the Club in deciding whether to join or not, you may have met the Membership Director, the General Manager, the Head Golf Professional, Food and Beverage Manager and so on. These are the first people you'll meet, maybe the only people you know at the Club, and we would drop in on them when coming to the Club to say "hi" and because we didn't know anyone else. These people will help you tremendously, they will go out of their way to introduce you to members they think you might get along with and they will be sure to give you tips about the goings on at the Club that you might want to attend too.

I RARELY GET AGGRAVATED at my Club because I'm pretty good at just following Rule Number 1 and keeping it simple that way. However, I do on occasion witness or hear about someone treating a Staff member poorly and that really doesn't sit well with me.

RULE NUMBER 3 - Choose to Be Positive *(you already won the lottery of life by being here in the first place)*

If you are looking for things that are right, you will surely find them. If you're looking for things that are wrong, you will surely find those too. So, what are you looking for? I hope it's not stuff to complain about or things that could be improved. For some, that's their nature. They notice stuff that's wrong and can't switch it off. But at your Club, let it go for the most part. It's not your job to fix everything or anything at all for that matter.

. . .

YOU'VE ARRIVED at your Club through some combination of hard work and good fortune. No reason to be a "Negative Nelly" at this point. Always be looking for the bright side, be quick to praise and slow to criticize. Sometimes there's a bit of a quandary between maintaining high standards and just picking your spots if you have a complaint/suggestion. If the service in the restaurant is a little slower than you like, so what. Just chill. Is it worth griping about? On the other hand, if someone has been rude and out of line, you don't have to put up with that. If you do have something that needs to be brought to the attention of the Staff to address, be careful to have that conversation in the tone that the situation calls for.

IT'S a fine line between knowing that things can't get fixed if the Staff doesn't know there's a problem and being a serial complainer. Usually, it's in the tone and the frequency. Choose wisely and don't be a buzzkill for your fellow members by complaining all the time. There is a saying that misery loves company and is that what you really want? To be in the company of other people who like to complain too?

ONE BIT of advice from my years on the Board would be that if you have a suggestion or a complaint or concern, take the time to put it in writing in an email. For some reason, random verbal input was less likely to be properly dealt with. If it came to me in an email, it was more likely to get the proper attention as it was already in a format to share the input with the people who could address it and very importantly, get back to the person who had taken the time to write it down.

RULE NUMBER 4 - Don't Be Cheap

Go out of your way to buy your golf items at your Club.

There is a time and place for bargain shopping but for the most part, get your stuff at your Club. There are bargains at your Club as well from time to time. Sometimes your Club may have limited inventory, but they can order most anything you need. As an example, we have tried on golf shoes at mega-stores, found what we like, taken a photo of the box and sent it to our own golf shop to order for us. Same for golf clubs, gloves and golf balls. Doesn't have to be 100% of the time, if you see a bargain somewhere on golf balls, go for it, but as a rule, check the box that says you go out of your way to buy your stuff from your own Club.

SOME CLUBS HAVE a no tip policy. If your Club is not one of those, then be generous. We have an 18% automatic gratuity for food and beverage at our Club. That doesn't seem like it's quite enough, so add a little more each time. I've heard people complain about that 18% if they happen to have poor service that time. It's not an audition by the server each time you're there to determine if they deserve a tip or not. Don't be cheap. If there's a service issue to be fixed, it won't happen by withholding a tip. If it's a consistent problem, let the appropriate person know in a respectful manner.

RULE NUMBER 5 - Be Aware of a Few Common Pitfalls

We're just here to have fun, make some friends and play some golf. But even something that simple can be screwed up. It seems to be human nature to complicate things that are not complicated. We've all seen it and here's a few of those pitfalls to be aware of:

TAKING Cheap Shots at Events and Their Organizers
- When you play in events, there has been a lot of planning

behind the scenes, countless decisions have been considered by the Staff or by Volunteers on Committees. You can't please everyone, so you make your best choices and go with it. It is stressful. Then someone takes a cheap shot, and you start to boil. Someone invariably will start to gripe about the food choice and yes, at that point you may flashback to the snob picture in your mind about what Club Membership might have been before joining. It's happened to both Sheri and I and it really is tough to get those incidents out of your mind. Frankly, you can't help but think a little less of those people. That seems to be human nature too. If you didn't step up to plan it and make the decisions, then it may be best to not complain. Not one word. If there is something that you absolutely must provide input on, take a moment to respectfully give your input in writing

Not Checking Your Ego at the Parking Lot

- You're successful at some level or you would not be at your Club. You're probably in charge of something and have a lot of decision-making responsibility at your day job. You may have position and status. Don't try to translate that to your Club. Nobody cares and it only makes you look ridiculous if you try to big-time your way around your golf club. That almost never happens at our Club, but it would not surprise me if it is happening to some degree in others. This is the place to get over yourself, it should be a relief that this is where you can let all that go and let your hair down a little.

Undermining your Board or Staff People

- If you have a beef about something, take it to the right people. Human nature is to complain to your group and try to get them to agree with you about whatever you see as wrong. Don't let that last for long, either let it go or take it to a decision maker. Otherwise, you could cause a rift in your Club and create factions that are hard to undo. I've seen people get so hardened in their positions and their factions that they had to leave the Club potentially just to do something as petty as saving face. By the time it got to that point, it was best for all that they just go away. Don't start down that path, for everyone's sake.

• Not using the word "we" instead of "they". There is no "they" at a golf Club. There is only "we". It's subtle but try to use the words "we" should consider adding this to the menu instead and see how that tone is much, much better. It's your club, so who is "they" anyway?

RULE NUMBER 6 - About Alcohol

Here we go. Sometimes alcohol is a big part of all that fun we were talking about. That said, know who you are and if you're overdoing it enough to be interfering with someone else's good time, try not to cross that line too often. Everyone gets a mulligan or two or three here, but after that, you might need to check yourself. If you have friends, they need to tell you. If you're one of those friends, you need to tell them. They know already but a nudge from a good friend might be a much-needed reminder to them.

RULE NUMBER 7 - Play In the Big Events

Try your best to make room in your calendar for your Club's big events. Make room where you can for any events for that matter but especially the big events. Those might be the tournaments like the Member/Guest, the Member/Member, the Club Championship. My calendar has caused me to be hit and miss on these from time to time and every time I play one, I swear I will never miss another. These events are the fabric and big part of the culture of the Club. They create camaraderie and great memories and bonding. There are usually great stories coming from these events that you want to be a part of or witness to.

And don't worry about the money (don't be cheap) or if your golf game is up to snuff. Just go with it and you'll be glad you did.

Rule Number 8 - Connect on Social Media

A good way to build community and stay connected can be through use of social media. It's a great way to keep up with friends and to have things to talk about when you do get face to face again. Post pictures of your vacations and take a little time to comment on your friend's posts as well. It helps you find things in common such as travel, hobbies, etc.

There are many downsides to social media these days as well, but I personally have found that sticking to the good side and avoiding the negative side, is still well worth it.

Rule Number 9 - Find a Few Regular Golf Buddies

One of the best ways to take your experience at your Club up several notches is to have a few regular golf buddies. They likely will come from part of larger regular groups that you play with, but they will be the people you must look forward to having a game with. These people could wind up being who you start to take trips and vacations with as well.

Rule Number 10 - Do Business with your Fellow Club Members Where Appropriate

Be proactive in doing business with fellow Club Members if you don't have a policy against such a thing. Don't be afraid to ask the staff or your fellow Members for recommendations on a variety of services such as medical, household, mortgage, real estate, and legal assistance. I so appreciate the people that work diligently for us in various areas like legal, medical, insurance, and so on. It's just such a great feeling to work with people and know that they care about you on another level, being that you are a fellow Club Member.

I KNOW that regardless of how business matters turn out, that at least they were doing their best on our behalf. It has not always been perfect and sometimes that can get awkward but most of the time it will go well and that makes it worth it. We've had a few Club Members help us with some important matters and they provided us such peace of mind in moments of high stress that it made an impression that will last a lifetime. Thank you to everyone at our Club who has been there when we needed you and to those who sent a caring note during a traumatic time for our family. You all know who you are, and we are so grateful for even the smallest gestures that have come our way. We love you!

4

PHOTOGRAPHS AND MEMORIES

One of my all time favorite pictures of Ally and Megan. Top of a double decker bus in Edinburgh Scotland....and I wouldn't have it but for a bucket list golf trip we decided to take.

Megan at Kingsbarns

Kingsbarns. Some say it's the Pebble Beach of Scotland. Great caddy, a kid on the St Andrews Golf Team

Halfway to Palm Desert, overnight in Lone Pine. Golf travel with friends is the best!

A good friend walking the course in Palm Desert, probably needed a break from us 😊

Somersett Pro Stuart Smith with his son Parker on the bag. When he's not busy running the worlds greatest Junior Golf Program, he's teeing it up in the PGA Championship!

*And that's how you qualify for the PGA Championship at Kiawa
Island. Somersett has the best Pro in the business*

*Ally and Megan walking off the first tee at The Old Course.
Nothing like this feeling anywhere. If you're a golfer, you must go*

The Open Championship at Carnoustie. We were on our way to Glenfiddich Distillery that day and just stopped by to be a tourist for a bit. On the list to visit and play in the future!

Great group at Sheep Ranch. Don't let the blue sky fool you, we played a bit in sideways rain and were rewarded with some sunshine for sticking it out!

One of my favorite views at Old Mac, top of the hill on the 3rd fairway

Sheri and her caddy on 16 at Bandon

Nothing quite like watching your kids enjoy this game together. 3rd tee at Bandon, probably my favorite par 5 anywhere

Here's a kid that's always going to be ok in this world. A picture is worth a thousand words and I literally could write more than that over all that I see here. Top 5 photo favorite photo for sure.

Rick Greene, RGB, Hall of Famer for all of us. Putting this trip together for 5 days with 32 guys for all these years. Thank you!

When you take golf travel trips with friends, this happens too! Zion National Park. Be sure to play Sand Hollow Golf Course if you're in the area.

5

**BUILDING RELATIONSHIPS WITH
CLUB MEMBERS**

I MENTIONED EARLIER THAT I TEND TO GET ALONG WELL WITH golfers in general, but I would jump at the chance to help a fellow Member of our Club.

ONCE YOU ARE at your Club for a while, you will start to figure out who you really get along with and want to hang out with. Some of these people will become part of the fabric of your lives…and your life will be immeasurably better because of it.

INVITES TO PEOPLE'S Homes
• Something happens when you have people over to your house and you visit others in their homes. People are trusting you. Trusting you not to be critical of them or how they live. Not to be critical of how they decorate or choose not to decorate. Trusting you enough to let them see the real you. When people trust you and think highly enough of you to invite you into their home, it makes you feel special. Some people are good at entertaining in their homes. They love it, they like to make the effort,

are generous by nature and are good at it. If they invite you, then enjoy it! If you are not as comfortable as those people, however, don't let that stop you. Just invite people over, be yourself and if someone is critical then that's their problem and certainly not yours. I can assure you we don't "entertain" in our home, but we love to have people over. Spontaneously right after a round of golf is my favorite, in part because there are no expectations, no anticipation to fret about, no one must navigate the "what can I bring" dynamic. Just finish the round and stop over for a beer and whatever snacks we can muster up. The best!

PARTIES

• It turns out grown people like to throw parties still! We've been to some memorable ones for sure with people in our Club. Raging New Year's Eve parties, Prime Rib dinner style New Year's Eve parties, Halloween Parties, Ice Cream Socials, Mid-Summer backyard Parties, lots of Christmas Parties and so on. Many of these are annual traditions and the people who do them are amazing for opening their homes for these bashes. I can assure you; everyone appreciates you for doing it, we all look forward to these more than you know, and they are so good for the soul to be able to gather with friends like this. For those of you throwing these parties, as big a hassle as they may be for you, we appreciate you! Uber in and Uber out if you think you need to.

WHAT ARE your other hobbies to be able to include Members in?

• Some of our best friends share common interests in Wine. Trips to wine country are a joy to plan for ahead of time, to enjoy while there and to savor the memories together for years afterwards.

• We have some good friends who were the instigators of my

bike hobby now. My friend had his bike with him on a Wine trip we made together and when he took off in the morning for a bike ride through wine country, I could not help but think that would be amazing! Fast forward a few years and we now travel with our bikes quite a bit and take in the sights while experiencing travel in a totally different and enjoyable way.

The Magic of Travel Together

• There's just so much to love about getting a chance to travel with friends. The planning and excitement leading up to the trip seem to be a big part of the fun. Having something to look forward to like that is hard to explain but we absolutely love the run-up to our trips. Go somewhere and enjoy the experience together. If Golf itself is a fast-forward button of sorts for getting to know people, then traveling together with golfers would be a turbo charger.

Be an Organizer

• We have a guy in our Club who is in the Organizer Hall of Fame for an awful lot of us. He puts together a trip every other year to Bandon Dunes, Oregon for 32 guys. This must be an enormous hassle. The fact that he puts this trip together with accommodations, tee times, restaurant reservations, etc. and all we need to do is show up and have a good time, is very much appreciated.

• We've had friends organize small group trips here and there and invite us along. We can't tell you how amazing it is to be invited and included in stuff like this. If you happen to feel a little left out from time to time on some things you know that your fellow members are doing but you have not been invited to, I'd say mostly it's a matter or proximity and spontaneous planning that starts these ideas and it's not personal if you're wondering what happened to your invite. If you feel like you're missing out a bit, just organize it yourself with friends that you have at your Club and those friends will wind up being even better friends.

• I guess a little advice if you are traveling with people is to be as flexible as humanly possible and don't get stuck on things being done your way or the way you are used to doing things. Just relax, enjoy and go with it wherever the "wind happens to blow" on your trip. If you want to go on a trip in your style and doing things your way all the time, then you should probably just go by yourself.

CLIQUES and About Feeling a Bit Left Out...

• Not everyone's job at the Club is to be an ambassador of sorts with new Members. There are many who informally do this because they want to help and are good at it. But most will not see themselves as having the responsibility to make you feel welcome. When you join a Club, the people who are already there have a head start in making friends and relationships. Don't take it personally. Maybe these people have been friends for years, have been to each other's homes, been on trips together, have seen their kids grow up together, may have been there for each other during very hard personal times and have played countless rounds of golf together and are very good friends. That doesn't make them "cliquey". They just have friends, that's all, and that is to be appreciated more than anything. As a Board Member, I used to hear that criticism from time to time and honestly, I have to say it became a self-fulfilling prophesy for them. They could become a little resentful, and people could feel it, which made it less likely that people would want to hang out with them, which made them more resentful and then less appealing to be around and so on...and then they would leave the club. Don't be jealous that people already have fast friends at the Club, that's what you're there for too. They just had a head start, that's all. Give it time and you too may be accused of being "cliquey" because you have a few friends at some point!

6

THE REAL GUIDE TO GOLF COURSE ETIQUETTE

"Play fast and don't be a Jerk" *Curtis Chan*

"Nobody cares" *Rich Engelen*

"Be a guy that everyone wants to play with" *Advice from Lauren O'Kane to Neil O'kane prior to joining the Club*

WE ALL KNOW THE RULES OF GOLF ETIQUETTE, RIGHT? DON'T STEP on someone's line on the putting green, don't talk during your playing partners back swing, be ready when it's your turn, take off your hat and shake hands after the round and so on and so forth. Those are the easy ones, the low hanging fruit so to speak. But those are just table stakes. If you want to have people want to keep playing golf with you, better get to know the real Etiquette, the annoying stuff, and the good stuff. It's a long and subtle list, maybe that's why golf is such a connectors game, because there actually *is* a lot going on and if you can navigate it, you will have golf buddies. It's a weird phenomenon, everybody knows these issues but will almost never call someone out on it and if you are the offender, don't count on someone bringing it to your attention. They will just hate on you in silence or talk about you at the bar afterwards. Yikes. Pay attention here...

HERE WE GO, in no particular order:

1. "NOBODY CARES"- Thank you Rich Engelen for this one. As social as Golf is, there is still a tendency to be totally immersed in your own golf game. Yes, you're in a group and trying to be considerate of certain things around your foursome but no one really cares that much about how you are doing. It's not personal, they are all focused intently on their own game. With that in mind, there is no need to be self-conscious about how you are playing. I repeat, no one cares about your golf game travails today on the golf course. So, whatever you do, don't talk too much about whatever it is you are going through during your round. At least as it pertains to golf. Other life stuff may be fair game, but no one wants to hear much more than a comment or two about how you are fighting your slice or about your weight transfer or whatever swing thoughts you've got going on. Your responsibility is to suffer in silence like the rest of us with the occasional (I repeat, occasional) swear word outburst for comedic effect at your frustration (that everyone understands), but nothing technical about your swing. You might not get invited back.

2. "NOBODY CARES" after your round either. Except maybe your spouse. After the round, nobody cares about how or what you did on the course. It's a common phrase when you see someone after your round to hear "how was your round?", they might not mean it. They just didn't know what else to say. Whatever you do, if someone asks, "how'd you do?", a short and sweet answer is best. A simple "it was golf.." or "couldn't buy a putt" or "good

thing the beer cart was running today.." and if you played well "surprisingly well" will do. I've been buried for 5 minutes by a shot-by-shot filibuster about someone's round of golf on more than one occasion and it's not pleasant to be on the receiving end of those. Unless you got a hole-in-one, or maybe an Eagle, they really do not want to hear much about it and are sorry immediately that they asked if you proceed to describe more than 1 or 2 shots in your round. And you might get avoided in the bar next time.

3. If it's not a tournament that requires you to hole out on every hole, don't be afraid to pick your ball up if you're getting your max score anyway. It happens to everyone, better to just own it. Everyone understands and they will appreciate it. If you're in the right group, you may not be the only one that day picking up on a hole, or a few holes if it's a particularly miserable day for you. People will note how you handle adversity (if you make them) and if your way of handling it is to be inconsiderate of others and insist on hitting that 3rd ball out of the whatever predicament you've gotten yourself into again, that would be frowned upon. And you might not get invited back.

4. Play fast and don't be a jerk. Best golf advice of all time. Thank you, Curtis Chan! It's not complicated, but here are some details one should be able to execute:

- Be ready when it's your turn. That means if it is humanly possible for you to have known your approximate yardage, have a club in hand and get to your ball, then do it. If it's your turn, hit the ball. You have to know, AT ALL TIMES, if you are going to be next after the person whose turn it is now. It's not complicated and you're not in a PGA Tour event. Step up and hit your ball.

- You do not have to know if it's 145 yards or 147 yards, you're not that accurate anyway. Get an idea of the yardage, guess a little on the wind impact and hit it. No amount of practice swings, staring at the ball, or thinking about what you're supposed to do is going to help. Just hit it already.

- If you lose a ball, the rules of golf allow 3 minutes to look for it. The unwritten rules of golf say that you get to do that maybe once or twice in a round. If you're having one of those days where you're looking for your ball a lot, spare everyone the headache, take a brief look for 10 seconds and then move it along. Taking 3 minutes every other hole or so and forcing your group into search party mode gets old quick.

- Walk around to eyeball your putt BEFORE it's your turn. If you're not first to putt and then when it becomes your turn, THEN you walk to the opposite side of the cup to take a look..well, that's just not ok and you should be banned from the course.

- If you just pay attention the little things like this, you should never feel rushed at all on a golf course while maintaining a good pace. If you feel rushed to keep up during a round, someone in your group is violating the unwritten Etiquette. If you can't identify who it is, then it's you! And you might not get invited back.

- When you leave the green and get to your cart, drive off right away if there is a group behind you waiting. Write your score down at the next hole. You can even put your clubs away at the next hole as well instead of hanging around the green to do so. If you're sitting in your cart trying to count all your strokes to write down before you drive away from the green, then you might have an incoming wayward shot come

bouncing past you from time to time. If you do, don't
blame the group behind you....

5. Which is worse, talking while someone is in their backswing
or having "Rabbit Ears" while someone is talking during your
backswing? The debate rages on. While it is correct that you are
not to talk during someone's backswing, there is backlash
behavior that you need to avoid as well. Yes, Rabbit Ears, we're
talking about you here. I submit to you that the only thing worse
than talking during someone's backswing is being above a zero
handicap that can't hit the ball if someone is having a conversation within your earshot. It's a social game and sometimes it just
happens that people are talking. Seriously, just hit the ball
whether someone is talking or not. If you hit a bad shot while
someone is talking, they will be apologizing all over themselves
anyway. But if you back off and give them the "you need to be
quiet in order for me to hit this ball" look, then you become the
one who is out of line. You're not on Tour, there's not a $2
Million first prize at stake, just hit the ball already whether
someone is talking or not. So yes, pay attention and try to stop a
conversation when someone is hitting. Be flexible if you're the
one hitting. Talking and/or conversations sometimes happen
and it's not a big deal, unless you're going to be a jerk about it.
And you might not get invited back.

6. Learn a few gambling games and use them where appropriate.
Always bring cash to the golf course, for tips and gambling.
Venmo has become acceptable to settle bets too, so get a Venmo
account. For some, it's not even Golf if there's not a little something riding on it. If the stakes aren't too high, just go with it and
partake. You'll be glad you did. It will make you a better player
and if you like adrenaline, you'll get a good dose of it no matter

the stakes, even over that three-foot putt. There will be some who like the higher stakes games and if you're uncomfortable with that, you most likely won't be in that group anyway. They know who the gambling junkies are and tend to want to play together. Learn a few games that are for the masses. I won't try to describe theme here, use Google and look them up.

- $5 Nassau, or otherwise known as "front, back and total"
- COD, which stands for "Carts, Opposites and Drivers"
- Wolf

7. Music on the golf course is a more recent issue to learn to navigate. If you haven't run across this one yet, you most likely will. Lots of people these days like to have music in their carts and some even have portable speakers with then while walking. If you're in your regular group, then it's probably not an issue. If you're not, then error on the side of caution. Even if you've asked and they've said yes to your music, keep the volume low in your cart. If they want the volume up and they like your music, they will ask you to turn it up. Some people find it hard to hear a conversation when they are near the speakers. Some people who love music in general still prefer the quiet of the golf course.

7

YOUR CLUB PROFESSIONALS

I'M NOT QUITE SURE HOW THEY DO IT, BUT MOST EVERY PGA CLUB Professional I have ever met seems to have a way with people that is just different. I marvel at it, how one profession can be so consistently good at something that I am not entirely sure can be taught. Perhaps it can best be described as a unique culture. PGA Professionals are the stewards and keepers of the game of golf, and they seem to carry that professionalism and dignity with them most every day in how they conduct themselves.

THERE SHOULD BE a separate business school study on these men and women as to how they do it. Just about every company or organization I have been around promotes or talks about their culture, but it really stands out in certain places more than others. Golf itself, and the people who play it, has a certain culture to be sure.

I RECALL a story about Southwest Airlines being asked how they teach their people to be so different, so fun, so entertaining, so relaxed when the rest of the industry seems so uptight and not having an ounce of fun. Southwest's response to the question has stuck with me over the years and made me question many things in my business life. Southwest's response was "we can't teach that, we have to hire that". Maybe that's true, but then from there, they must cultivate and grow that special nature that these people bring to the table.

I WONDER if that is what happens with PGA Professionals. Maybe they are wired for it when they get there and then the PGA of America has a fantastic system to develop it from there. Don't get me wrong, there's a little Caddyshack comedy running in the background at every Pro Shop I've been in and they like to have fun in there. But when it matters, these people are the best. Treat your Club Professionals with admiration and respect for the role they play, what they do day in and day out and how they go about their business. My family is forever in their debt.

WE HAVE the best Club Professional in the business. I hope you feel that way about yours too, but we really do have the best one in the business! On behalf of the entire Club, thank you Stuart Smith.

PRO TIP:

If you are traveling, your Club Professional may be able to arrange for you to play at a guest fee rate at a nice Private Club at your destination. It's never a guarantee, but it's a nice professional courtesy between Clubs and the Pro's don't seem to mind doing this for you. If they happen to arrange a round for you on your trip, consider leaving a nice bottle of wine for the Pro at the Club you are visiting and one for your own Pro too when you get back. Again, it's not something you are entitled to, and it is never guaranteed, but it does make you feel special when it can be arranged.

8

BRINGING IT ALL TOGETHER

GOLF IS A MICROCOSM OF LIFE AND, IN PART, THAT'S WHY IT'S SO special. It can be a fast-forward button for relationships. You can assume A LOT when you meet a fellow golfer and after a few minutes, some of those assumptions are either confirmed or rejected. It's a study in human interaction.

IT'S a busy world out there and getting busier and busier all the time. Golf courses are sanctuaries from all of that and your mental health may thank you. Take a moment to breathe it in a little more during your next round. Just stop and take a good look at the scenery, feel the quiet, enjoy the walking, enjoy the camaraderie, and don't ever take it for granted.

MY COURSE IS BUILT for riding in a golf cart, but my ideal round is and always will be a walking round. Walking golf and riding golf are *not* the same. Go out of your way to play a course from time to time that allows you to walk the round.

· · ·

IF YOU HAVE THE CHANCE, occasionally, go late in the day for a few holes just by yourself or just hang around the chipping area and think, enjoy the solitude and work on your game a bit. It's a great place to think and reflect. Humans *think and reflect* better when we're moving.

IN A WAY, the modern world *needs* golf. We need a different type of dopamine delivery system than what we get from social media scrolling, 24/7 news feeds and what I heard called "the Outrage Industrial Complex" that is Political TV. The type of dopamine that is released when we feel the impact of a well struck golf ball and that *moment* in time when you look up to see it. In those moments, your mind is clear, there is not a worry in the world for you. You truly are *in the moment* and that is becoming more valuable than ever in our frantic, distracted, multitasking world that we live in.

IT'S ALWAYS BEEN a sanctuary and an escape for guys with stressful jobs. But now, all of society could use a break and a place to clear their heads. It's hard to *be present* and *free from distraction* these days, but it's more important than ever to find that space; one you might possibly find on a golf course.

ENJOY YOUR TIME on the course, the time with friends or by yourself, along with the time at your Club. Don't ever take your golf Club for granted and always appreciate it. Pay your dues and avoid any unnecessary sense of entitlement. Slow your life down for a few hours on a regular basis and breathe it in. Live in gratitude for all that the game and your Club bring to your lives. And be the person that everyone wants to play with.

Made in the USA
Monee, IL
16 February 2022

91044700R10036